THE BIBLE AND MODERN SCHOLARSHIP

THE BIBLE AND
MODERN SCHOLARSHIP

★　　★　　★

BY

Sir FREDERIC G. KENYON,

G.B.E., K.C.B., F.B.A.

*Formerly Director and Principal Librarian
of the British Museum*

★

LONDON

JOHN MURRAY, ALBEMARLE STREET, W.

First Edition	.	February	1948
Reprinted	.	April	1948
Reprinted	.	June	1948
Reprinted	.	September	1948
Reprinted	.	January	1949

Made and Printed in Great Britain by Butler & Tanner Ltd., Frome and London

In Memoriam

H. H. H.

fautoris huius opusculi

INTRODUCTION

THE foundation of the following essay was a lecture delivered by me before the University of London in November, 1947, as the first in a series of annual lectures on Biblical archaeology and criticism founded by Mrs. Ethel M. Wood, owner of a collection of Bibles destined for the University. It seemed suitable to choose as the subject of such an inaugural lecture the present position of archaeological and literary criticism in relation to the authenticity and authority of the books of which the Bible is composed, all the more because the discoveries of the last fifty years, and especially of the last fifteen, seem to me to have altered that position very materially. I believe that the time has come to re-assess the value of that criticism, to shake off the excessive scepticism characteristic of much Biblical scholarship in the latter part of the nineteenth century, and to restore confidence in the Bible as a guide to truth and a basis for the conduct of life.

The main substance of the lecture was accordingly a summary of the more important developments in archaeological discovery and literary criticism during (approximately) the present century; but I found it necessary to take particular notice of a book which appeared to reach, as the result of enlightened modern scholarship, conclusions exactly the opposite of those which I was maintaining. This was the work of the Bishop of Birmingham entitled *The Rise of Christianity*, the tenor of which was to discredit the authenticity of the books of the New Testament, to refer them in the main to dates well on in the second century, and consequently to weaken very seriously the reader's confidence in their accuracy as a record of the life and teaching of our Lord and His Apostles.   Such a challenge could not be ignored by anyone holding the views which I had endeavoured to state.   I have no liking for controversy, and least of all, for criticism of one who holds so honourable a position in the Church as Dr. Barnes ; but since a detailed examination of the Bishop's book had convinced me that it was no up-to-date representation of the results of modern scholarship, but, on the contrary, was a revival of a school of criticism which had some vogue about seventy years ago, and ignored almost wholly the results of the last fifty years, I felt that some demonstration of this was called for, lest the Bishop's position in the Church should be thought to give his opinions a weight which, from the point of view of scholarship, they did not seem to deserve.

The lecture therefore comprised both a constructive statement of what I believe to be the outcome of modern research and a criticism of the Bishop's book.   I had not at first thought of further publication of it : but I was strongly urged, from quarters which I was bound to respect, to make it available, in an expanded form, to a wider public.   It was represented to me that some sort of answer was desirable, on account of the mischief which such destructive criticism by a Bishop might do ; and that in view of Dr. Barnes's expressed depreciation of the value of criticisms by writers of his own cloth, such an answer would come better from a layman.   Dr. Barnes has a poor opinion of either the intellect or the honesty of those who, in his own words, " feel bound to reach conclusions prescribed by the Christian community to which they belong ".   He does not appear to realise that some of them may have formed their opinions before they took Holy Orders, while others, having taken Orders, may yet have retained their intellectual honesty. He does not seem to have been unduly hampered by these fetters himself ; and in any case it is somewhat cavalier treatment to apply to such scholars as Lightfoot, Westcott, Salmon, Sanday, Gore and many others. Still a layman, though not claiming to rank with these great names, may have his uses ; and I have accordingly consented to expand my lecture, as originally written, to its present form. The greater part of it will be a statement of the more recent developments of research and criticism ; a smaller part will be devoted to the vindication of the conclusions thus arrived at against the destructive criticism of Dr. Barnes's book.

In the account given of recent archaeology and criticism, I shall necessarily be covering ground with which I have dealt in previous writings [1] ; but I have no right to assume that those writings will be known to those who may read this booklet, and in any case it will be convenient to have the whole case laid connectedly before the reader. I can only hope that it may be of some assistance to those who look to Christianity as the one hope of our distracted world, and to the Bible as an assured foundation for the Christian belief.

---

[1] *The Bible and Archæology* (1940): *The Reading of the Bible* (1944). The former has been out of print for several years ; the latter deals with the subject briefly and sporadically.

BIBLICAL CRITICISM IN THE NINETEENTH CENTURY

THE main thesis of this essay is that in the study of the Bible we have passed from a primitive stage of unquestioning and sometimes unintelligent acceptance, through a period of criticism and doubt, sometimes sound but often hypercritical, to a position where we are entitled to claim that the best and most untrammelled scholarship can be shown to have vindicated its authenticity and its trustworthiness. A review of the development of thought and discovery during the nineteenth and twentieth centuries will, I believe, justify this contention. It is not, from the point of view here taken, a question of theology or of religious emotion, but of scholarship,—scholarship which has too often been invoked as a destructive agency, but which is indeed, if followed sanely and impartially, an agency of construction, leading to established confidence.

The Victorian Age was a period in which two different and incompatible attitudes to the Bible were in existence side by side. For the general public it was an age of Bible-reading and Churchgoing, when the Bible was normally accepted as it stood, unquestionable as history no less than as a guide to life, every word of which could be applied to any and every situation, without reference to its original date or context. The five books of the Pentateuch were commonly regarded as the work of Moses (though his authorship is nowhere claimed in them), and attempts were seldom made to analyse the composition of the other historical books. Nor was any discrimination made between the several periods of the story. The Bible was a revelation made once for all, and what was said in the days of Moses or the Judges was held applicable without question to the conditions of the nineteenth century.

On the other hand, for the scholar the nineteenth century was an age of growing criticism, in which everything was open to question and the foundations of learning were being digged up. This attitude of mind was not confined to the Bible. Criticism was in the air, and men looked with fresh eyes and inquiring interest on the settled convictions and accepted opinions of their ancestors. Indeed, the new spirit showed itself earlier in respect of classical than of Biblical studies. It was in 1795 that Wolf's *Prolegomena* launched what became notorious as " the Homeric question ", which assailed the unity of the Iliad (and eventually of the Odyssey), and dissolved " Homer " into a syndicate or succession of unknown authors and editors ; and even Wolf had a predecessor in Robert Wood in 1769. It was not until well on in the nineteenth century that the same spirit touched the criticism of the Bible, first in respect of the New Testament (which will be dealt with below) and then with respect of the Old.

Along with criticism from the side of literary analysis, another influence was at work which shook the complacence of accepted views. This was the progress of scientific discovery and the development of scientific methods of thought. It became clear that the cosmology of the book of Genesis could not be reconciled with the evidence of geology and astronomy. A further shock was given by the Darwinian doctrine of evolution, which disturbed the faith of many. In this heyday of scientific advance, when scientists honestly thought that the key of all problems was in their hands, the Bible inevitably lost much of its hold, especially on the young and intellectually enterprising.

In the case of the Old Testament, the critical attack

took the form of an analysis of the structure and composition of the several books. The discernment that the
Pentateuch is a composite structure, containing (most
notably in Genesis) duplicate narratives which have been
compounded by a later editor, goes back to the French
scholar Simon in 1678 ; and the idea was developed by a few
writers in the following century ; but it made no great im-
pact on scholars in general, and still less on the Bible-reading
public, until developed by Ewald and Graf in the sixties
of the nineteenth century, and especially in J. Wellhausen's
work on *The Composition of the Hexateuch* published in 1876.
In this country these views were introduced mainly by
W. Robertson Smith (*The Old Testament in the Jewish Church*,
1881, and articles in the *Encyclopaedia Britannica*, 9th edn.)
and S. R. Driver (*Introduction to the Literature of the Old
Testament*, 1891). These scholars and their followers pre-
sented to the world the view that the Pentateuch, instead of
being a single work, conventionally attributed to Moses and
therefore regarded as composed about 1400–1200 B.C.
according to the date assigned to the Exodus, was a composite structure, of which the main components were (1)
two narratives, known as J and E, written about the ninth
century in the kingdoms of Judah and Israel respectively,
(2) the book of Deuteronomy (D), substantially the Book
of the Law discovered in the Temple in the reign of Josiah
(621 B.C.), (3) the Priestly Narrative (P), composed in the
time, and perhaps by the hand, of Ezra (398 B.C.), the whole
being worked together into a continuous narrative about
that time.

This literary analysis was by itself sufficiently disturbing
to the traditional view of the Bible ; but it was lent much
more destructive weight by the prevalent belief that writing
was not known, or at any rate not used for literary purposes,
until well after 1000 B.C. In the *Encyclopaedia Britannica*

(9th edn., 1881), the origins of writing are placed about the eighth century; Grote, in 1846, assigns the beginning of written Greek literature to the middle of the seventh century; Wellhausen (*Encycl. Brit.*, s.v. "Israel") puts it in the century 850–750 B.C., contrasting the absence of records of the prophecies of Elijah and Elisha with the written book of Amos. If, then, the Pentateuch, instead of being written by Moses, represented at best traditions handed down orally over a period of some four hundred years, it would have very slight historical validity; and to this it was added that the legislation attributed to Moses was far more elaborate and detailed than could be supposed to have existed at that remote age. The position of the Old Testament as an authentic historical record was therefore severely shaken.

In the case of the New Testament, the critical attack may be dated from the writings of F. C. Baur and his "Tübingen School", beginning in 1831. This became an all-round attack on the integrity of the New Testament. Nearly all its books were declared to be unauthentic, i.e. they were not of the dates nor by the authors that tradition assigned to them. Baur started with a theory that the whole early history of Christianity centred on a supposed embittered hostility between Peter and Paul and their respective followers; and any early writing inconsistent with this hypothesis must be regarded as spurious. Of the epistles attributed to St. Paul, Romans, 1 and 2 Corinthians, and Galatians were allowed to stand, because they showed some signs of friction between Paul and the other Apostles; but all the other nine were ruled out. Acts also must go, since it represents Paul as on friendly terms with Peter and James, and receiving support from them. The first Epistle of Peter is too Pauline in doctrine to be genuine. With these go the earliest non-canonical writings, the epistles of

Clement, Ignatius and Polycarp. Further, all the Gospels are excluded from the Apostolic Age. The Synoptics are assigned to the first half of the second century, and the Fourth Gospel to the second half. Of all the New Testament, only the four Pauline epistles and the Apocalypse are allowed to remain in the first century.

Of the whole Tübingen theory of the Peter-Paul controversy not one shred is now accepted by responsible scholars ; but it started a phase of criticism which for two generations dominated thought and practice, notably in Germany and Holland, but with repercussions in this country, where Germany was generally regarded as the leader in intellectual activity, in Biblical as well as in classical scholarship. Naturally some scholars tried to out-Baur Baur. The Dutch school of van Manen expelled even the four Epistles which Baur had left with St. Paul : " They are all, without exception, pseudepigrapha. . . . No distinction can any longer be allowed between 'principal epistles' and minor or deutero-Pauline ones. The separation is purely arbitrary, with no foundation in the nature of the things here dealt with. The group, when compared with the Johannine epistles, with those of James, Jude, Ignatius, Clement, with the gospel of Matthew or the martyrdom of Polycarp, bears obvious marks of a certain unity, of having originated in one circle, at one time, in one environment, but not of unity of authorship, even if a term of years,—were it even ten or twenty—be allowed." All are " the later development of a school, or, if the expression is preferred, of a circle of progressive believers who named themselves after Paul and placed themselves as it were under his aegis " (van Manen, *Encyclopaedia Biblica*, iii. 3634). Similarly, in the same publication (ii. 1892–4) P. W. Schmiedel, of Zurich, concludes that, whatever value may be attached to Papias' statement that Mark wrote a Gospel, the Gospel which now bears his name is not the original Mark ; that Matthew may be as late as A.D. 130, but more probably was mainly in existence before 119 ; that Luke may be placed between 100 and 110, with Acts to follow ; and that John was produced between 132 and 140.

This represents in summary fashion the high-water mark of the school of destructive criticism which originated with the work of Baur. Its effect was to transfer to the second century the whole evidence with regard to the life of Christ and the growth of Christianity in the age of the Apostles, with the implication that none of it could be held to be beyond suspicion of partisan or propagandist manipulation, and every scholar was free to accept just so much or so little as suited the thesis which he adopted, and to ignore the rest as unauthentic. The result, apart from particular details, was the establishment of a wholly anti-traditional atmosphere. On every point of dispute there was a presumption that the tradition was wrong. The flimsiest argument against the tradition would be accepted in preference to substantial evidence in favour of it ; and no scholar would be regarded as intellectually abreast of his times if he maintained the general reliability of the tradition. If, as was sometimes contended, no scholar in England could look for advancement in the Church unless he were orthodox, it was equally true that no scholar in Germany could look for a professorship unless he was ' progressist '. If a discount was to be applied on the one side, it was equally applicable on the other.

This weight of attack, whether from the angle of science or from that of literary criticism, derived much of its effect from the fact that, as indicated above, it fell upon an attitude of mind with regard to the Bible which was peculiarly open to criticism. In the early days of Christianity possibilities of error and variations of interpretation were by no means excluded. Doubts as to the character and authority of certain books could be freely expressed when the limits of the canon had not been fixed, and criticism could be allowed a hearing. But since the Bible had become familiar to the English people in their own language, and especially since the rise and spread of Puritanism, it had acquired such a complete predominance that criticism was almost excluded. The inerrancy of the Bible had become almost an article of faith ; to question it in one point was to attack its authority in all. The attacks of criticism acquired additional strength from the intellectual inadequacy of the defence of such a position. If certain statements in the Bible narrative were incompatible with the results of modern research and scientific discovery, it was felt by some that its authority as an infallible guide to life, even in matters quite in-dependent of history or science, was shaken. The result was that, as the Victorian Age progressed, a generation was growing up which was being led to believe that the authority of the Bible was irreconcilable with scientific truth, and therefore could no longer be maintained. There followed, as a consequence, first, a decline in Bible-reading and in churchgoing, and, as the inevitable sequel, a loss of standards and a shaking of principles, of which we are now reaping the harvest.

In England, following rather belatedly behind German leadership, the climax of the sceptical movement may be found in the work of W. R. Cassels, *Supernatural Religion*, published in 1871–77, with an aftermath in the *Encyclopaedia Biblica* in 1899–1903. Cassels' work was originally pub-lished anonymously, and obtained a somewhat excessive vogue from reports that its author was in fact a bishop of the Church of England, Connop Thirlwall of St. David's, a distinguished scholar who was supposed to hold rather 'advanced' views. For these rumours there was no sort of foundation, but they contributed to give the book a vogue altogether out of proportion to its merits, and it went through several editions between 1874 and 1879. It was a thoroughgoing attack on the belief in miracles and on the date, authority and authenticity of the books of the New Testament, and from its appearance of scholarship it made a considerable impression.

Nevertheless, the best English scholars were not carried away by it, and by the end of the century the reaction had well begun. Bishop Lightfoot had brought to bear upon Cassels' work, in a series of articles in 1874–77, afterwards published as *Essays on the Work entitled Supernatural Religion* (1889), the artillery of a much sounder and more learned criticism, which in fact blew it to pieces. Others, such as Driver, Sanday, Salmon, Westcott and Hort, had shown the combination of common sense with learning which is characteristic of the best English work ; and their conclusions were wholly in favour of the general soundness of the tradition. Even on the Continent there was a strong trend in the same direction. The turn of the tide was definitely marked there by the declaration of Adolf Harnack in the preface to his monumental *Chronologie der altchristlichen Litteratur bis Eusebius* (1897, pp. viii–x) that "in all main points and in most details the earliest literature of the Church is, from a literary-historical point of view, trustworthy and dependable. In the whole New Testament there is apparently only one single writing which can be called pseudonymous in the strictest sense of the term, namely the Second Epistle of Peter . . . The assumptions of the school of Baur, one can almost say, are now wholly abandoned ; but there remains an indefinite lack of confidence in the criticism of the early Christian literature, a method which clings to all sorts of small details, which it seeks to use as arguments against the clear and decisive evidence . . . The chronological framework in which the tradition has arranged the documents is, in all the principal points, from the Pauline Epistles to Irenaeus, correct, and compels the historian to abandon all hypotheses with relation to the historical course of things that are inconsistent with this framework." Harnack was universally recognised as the foremost scholar of his time in Biblical criticism and early Christian history, and could certainly not be accused of a bias in favour of orthodoxy ; and, in spite of a belated recrudescence to which it will be necessary to refer later, his explicit declaration may be taken as marking the end of the vogue of the school of Baur. " That time ", as Harnack said, " is over. It was an episode during which science learnt much, and after which it must forget much."

2

DISCOVERIES AND CRITICISM IN THE TWENTIETH CENTURY

UNTIL about the last decade of the nineteenth century archaeological discovery had done little to affect either the earlier periods of Hebrew history or the textual criticism of the Greek Bible. Layard and Rassam had discovered at Nineveh the libraries of the Assyrian kingdom, with the records of Sennacherib's campaigns against Hezekiah, and the Assyrian version of the stories of the Creation and the Flood ; and the Moabite Stone (discovered in 1868) and the Siloam inscription (discovered in 1880) had provided early examples of Hebrew writing. Egyptian excavations had produced little with direct bearing upon Biblical subjects. From about 1890 onwards, however, there was a considerable change : and the discoveries of the last fifty years have very materially affected the criticism of both Testaments. These results must now be reviewed.

(a) OLD TESTAMENT

With regard to the Old Testament, the most fundamental change was produced by the transfer of archaeological research from the territory of Assyria in Upper Mesopotamia to the ancient cities of Babylonia in Lower Mesopotamia. There the American excavations at Nippur (1889-1900), of the Germans at Ashur (1903–14), of the British Museum and the University of Pennsylvania at Ur (1918–39), of Oxford and Chicago at Kish (1922–26), with much sporadic and unregulated digging by natives, especially at

Lagash, brought to light thousands of inscribed tablets ranging back to the third millennium B.C. Most of these were business documents, but many also were literary or semi-literary, and they established beyond question the antiquity and general use of writing from an age far preceding that of Abraham. Writings nearly as old have appeared on papyrus rolls discovered in Egypt, with presumptive evidence carrying back the use of writing still further. Still more recently excavations have been proceeding in various parts of Syria between the Mediterranean and Mesopotamia, and also in eastern Asia Minor. These resulted in the discovery of the archives of the Hittite Empire, ranging from the fourteenth century B.C., at Boghaz-Keui in northern Cappadocia, of the Canaanite kingdom of Ugarit, at Ras Shamra near Alexandretta, from about the fifteenth to the end of the thirteenth century, and of collections of tablets from various other sites, such as Atchana (north of Ras Shamra), Byblos (on the Mediterranean coast, south of Beirut), Mari (on the middle Euphrates), Tell Halaf and Chagar Bazar (between the Euphrates and Tigris in northern Assyria), and Kirkuk and Nuzi (east of the Tigris). All of these belong to the second millennium B.C., and with them may be classed the Tell el-Amarna tablets discovered in Egypt in 1887 and comprising the correspondence of the governors of cities in Syria and Palestine (including Jerusalem) with their Egyptian overlords in the first half of the fourteenth century; and the yet undeciphered tablets of the Minoan kingdom in Crete. These discoveries have made it abundantly clear that writing, both for business and for literary purposes, was fully and freely practised from the middle of the second millennium (and in some places much earlier); and that when the Israelites left Egypt they came from a country where writing had been in use for several centuries to a country in which it was equally known and practised by the Amorite or Canaanite inhabitants and by their neighbours in Syria, Mesopotamia and Asia Minor. It is therefore no longer legitimate to argue that the writers who composed the books which we know as the Pentateuch had not at their disposal written records contemporary with Moses, and possibly even earlier, since writing was well known at Ur of the Chaldees when Abraham left it.

A special application of this relates to the legislation of the Pentateuch. It was formerly maintained that laws so elaborate as these were inconceivable in the age of Moses and could not have been handed down in the form of so detailed a code. This assumption has been explicitly disproved by two particular discoveries. In 1901–2 French excavations at Susa discovered a great column, containing the laws of Hammurabi, king of Babylon, whose reign is now assigned to the years 1792–1750 B.C. Here is the original code of laws of the kingdom of Babylon (from which the column was transferred to Susa by a later Elamite conqueror), ranging, as now edited, to 282 clauses, fully as elaborate in detail and often similar in their provisions to the legislation in Leviticus. Closer still are the laws of the Hurri or Horites of about 1400 B.C., discovered by an American expedition at Kirkuk and Nuzi in 1922 and later, which include provisions for the marriage of a childless widow to her brother-in-law and for the right of daughters to inherit, when there was no male heir, exactly corresponding to the Mosaic legislation on these points. It may still be legitimate to argue that certain particular provisions in the Pentateuch are later additions, but it is not permissible to assume that a detailed code of laws could not have been compiled in the time of Moses and handed down in written form.

The discoveries at Ras Shamra (1929 and onwards) are of special significance for Old Testament history. Many of the tablets bear the name of Nigmed, king of Ugarit about the middle of the second millennium B.C.; and most of them are religious texts, which give us first-hand knowledge of the religion of the Canaanites at the time of the Israelite invasion. It is a polytheistic religion, having El as its chief god, with Asherat as his consort and Baal as his son and the most prominent deity in Canaanite worship. It is indeed the religion of Baal of which we hear so much in the history of the kingdoms of Israel and Judah, and which was the rival of the religion of Jehovah until the days of the Captivity. It is a religion not without its beauty and poetry, which offers some parallels with Hebrew beliefs; but the differences are more marked. Its polytheism, with the stories of conflicts between the various deities, their deaths and revivals and their deeds of violence, contrasts strongly with the Hebrew monotheism of the worship of Jehovah. So far from providing an origin for Hebrew religion, it brings out the superiority of the latter even before the period of the great prophets and still more after that.

Another subject on which recent discoveries have thrown some light, though the conclusions to be drawn are not yet quite certain, is the date of the Exodus and the Hebrew invasion of Palestine. There are two alternative dates for the Exodus, the first half of the fourteenth century or the second half of the thirteenth. In favour of the latter is the name Raamses applied to one of the cities built by the Hebrews in Egypt (Exodus i, 11). This seemed to point to a date in or after the reigns of the Rameses Dynasty, and it was usual to assign the Exodus to the reign of the son of Rameses II, Merenptah (1233–23). Recent discoveries, however, appear to favour the earlier date. An inscription of Merenptah was found at Thebes in 1896, containing a song of triumph over the king's enemies, including the Hittites, Canaanites, Philistines and Israelites:

" Israel is desolated, her seed is not : Palestine has become a defenceless widow for Egypt." This seems to imply that by the time of Merenptah the Israelites were already settled in Palestine. Then the Tell el-Amarna letters and some of the Ras Shamra literature indicate a period of disturbance in Palestine, with an irruption of invaders who are called ' Terachites ' or ' Habiru '; and though the latter term occurs elsewhere in a wider connotation than the Hebrews, it cannot be denied that it may have included them and ultimately have been attached specifically to them. Finally, the excavations of Professor Garstang at Jericho (1929 onwards), if rightly interpreted by the excavator (which some dispute),[1] indicate a destruction in the early fourteenth century which responds remarkably to the narrative in the book of Joshua : double walls and houses on them, destruction as by an earthquake followed by fire, then a long period of non-occupation, followed by renewed residence on a smaller scale. All this seems to fit in with the earlier date for the Exodus though it is not yet unquestionably decisive.

Excavations at Jerusalem, Samaria, Bethshan and Megiddo have contributed some details to the history of the Israelite kingdoms ; but the greater results are those already indicated. The early use of writing is established beyond question ; and the use of early documents by the eventual

---

[1] It is much to be desired that this doubt should be cleared up ; for if (as seems increasingly probable) the destruction of Jericho can be assigned to the first half of the fourteenth century, its close correspondence to the narrative in Joshua (the city violently destroyed and a long period of non-occupation) would appear to fix the date of the Hebrew invasion, and consequently of the Exodus. The evidence of the Tell el-Amarna letters and the Ras Shamra documents as to the disturbed state of Palestine and the irruption of invaders would then fall naturally into place. It all turns on the dating of the pottery found in the Jericho excavations.

authors of the Pentateuch as we have it has become possible, and therefore probable. Further, the whole Hebrew story has acquired a background in our knowledge of the surrounding peoples in Egypt, Babylonia, Assyria, with the Hittites, the Amorites and the Hurri. We can read it now in a fuller perspective, and can follow more intelligently the growth of religion among the Hebrews, through the great prophets and the better kings, amid the constant rivalry of the Canaanite worship of Baal.

But in addition to the great increase in knowledge thus obtained, we have learnt a method of studying and understanding the Old Testament greatly superior to the uncritical methods of earlier generations, when knowledge was less and the materials for criticism which we now possess had not come to light. To put it briefly, we can abandon the "fundamentalist" doctine of the inerrancy of Scripture not merely without harm to its religious authority, but with a positive reinforcement of it. Instead of an indiscriminate application of texts of Scripture without reference to their date or context, we can regard the Old Testament as the record of a continuous and progressive training of a chosen people from the elementary monotheism of a particular family and tribe amid polytheistic surroundings, with its primitive legends and imperfect moral standards, up to the declaration by the great prophets in the earlier period of the Israelite and Judaite kingdoms of the universality of Jehovah's rule and the moral standards required by Him, and so on to the ultimate revelation of His nature embodied in the New Testament. From this point of view we need no longer be distressed by the incompatibility of primitive Hebrew science with the science of Copernicus and Newton, which the Hebrews could not know, and we can understand that lower standards of morality, as in respect of polygamy and the slaughter of enemies, might be permissible as the Hebrews were gradually raised from the standards of their neighbours ; we can welcome the freest application of scholarship to their records, though without necessarily accepting the last word of every new adventurer in Biblical study : and with all this acceptance of modern scholarship and research we can see that the moral value of the Old Testament is in no way impaired, but rather is illuminated and enhanced.

(b) NEW TESTAMENT

When we turn to the New Testament, the field is narrower in point of time, and the subject is mainly the dates and trustworthiness of the books included in it.   But here again the general effect of modern criticism and discovery is the same, the refutation of extravagant anti-traditional specula-tions and the re-establishment of the main lines of the tradition with fuller knowledge and on a securer basis.   We are concerned more with manuscripts and textual theories than with archaeology, though it should be observed that in many small details, especially in respect of the narrative of St. Paul's journeys in Acts, modern discovery has again and again established the author's accuracy where critics had been inclined to question it.

The main advance has been due to the discovery in Egypt of portions, sometimes small and sometimes substantial, of papyrus manuscripts of the New Testament earlier than those previously known.   When the Revised Version of the New Testament was published in 1881, simultaneously with the revised Greek text edited by Westcott and Hort, both were based in the main on the two great fourth-century manuscripts, the Vaticanus and the Sinaiticus, of which the latter had been discovered and the former more adequately made known by Tischendorf within the previous twenty years.   These manuscripts dated from the very beginning

of the period when vellum was adopted as the principal
material of book-production. Before that there was a gap,
which seemed unlikely to be filled, owing to the perishability
of papyrus, the book material in general use through the
Graeco-Roman world. This gap has been to a great
measure filled by discoveries within the present century.
Papyrus manuscripts containing documents and literary
works in the Greek language first came to light so far back
as 1778, but for a century from that date the discoveries
were few and sporadic, and (with the exception of thirty-two
leaves of a Psalter written in the seventh century, and
therefore of minor importance) had no bearing on the Bible.
It was not until 1877 that any large quantity of documents
were brought to light, and it is only since 1891 that a rich
supply of works of literature, as well as thousands of non-
literary documents, began to flow from Egypt to the libraries
and museums of Europe and America. Even so there was
at first little of Biblical interest. There were portions of
Genesis and the Psalter, of the fourth century, and of
Zephaniah and Malachi, of the seventh, but of the New
Testament nothing but a considerable part of the Epistle
to the Hebrews, in a hand of the late third or early fourth
century, written on the back of a roll containing an Epitome
of Livy. More interesting than this were two fragments,
one a leaf from a codex, the other a portion of a roll (both
of the third century) of a collection of Sayings of our Lord.
Some of these repeat in varying forms words known to us
in the canonical Gospels ; one is quoted by Clement of
Alexandria as from the Gospel according to the Hebrews ;
others are new, and generally have a somewhat mystical
character, similar to some which are found in early Christian
writings, but of which the genuineness can be neither proved
nor disproved. They have, however, no bearing on the
authenticity or text of the New Testament books.

The first really important discovery of Biblical manuscripts did not appear till 1931. This was a group consisting of portions (sometimes substantial, sometimes small) of eleven codices (*i.e.* in leaves like a modern book, not rolls) ranging in date from the second to the fourth century and therefore for the most part older than the great vellum codices, the Vaticanus and Sinaiticus, which up to then were the oldest extant authorities for the text of the Greek Bible. The greater part of the find was acquired by Mr. A. Chester Beatty, and they are therefore generally known as the Chester Beatty papyri : but substantial portions also went to the universities of Michigan and Princeton.

Of these eleven manuscripts, seven contained portions of the Septuagint version of the Old Testament: two of Genesis, one of the third century and the other of the fourth, containing between them the greater part of the book, and all the more valuable because the book is almost wholly lacking in the Vaticanus and Sinaiticus MSS.; one with large portions of Numbers and Deuteronomy, of the first half of the second century; one of Isaiah, comprising fragments of 33 leaves in a large and fine hand of the third century; two small portions of Jeremiah, of the end of the second century; fifty leaves (out of a probable total of 118) of a codex of the first half of the third century, the first half of which contained the book of Ezekiel, and the second (in a different hand) those of Daniel and Esther, the Daniel being particularly important because it contains the original Septuagint text, otherwise known only from one Greek and one Syriac manuscript, the Septuagint translation having been superseded in general use by that of Theodotion; and a leaf and a half of a fourth-century codex of Ecclesiasticus. Three manuscripts are of the New Testament, among which nearly every book is represented; one having originally contained the four Gospels and Acts in a hand which may be assigned to the first half of the third century ; one contains nearly the whole of the Pauline Epistles (86 leaves out of 104, of which the last five were probably blank), written about A.D. 200 ; and one with the middle third of Revelation of the third century. The remaining manuscript in the collection is non-canonical, containing the latter part of the book of Enoch and a homily by Melito, bishop of Sardis in the second half of the second century, on the Passion.

It will be seen that these manuscripts between them carry back the textual tradition of the New Testament for a full century. The Gospels and Acts manuscript is very imperfect, consisting of thirty leaves, nearly all incomplete, out of a probable total of 110 ; but the handwriting is very small, so that, except in the case of St. Matthew, enough is preserved to show clearly the character of the text. This character is highly interesting and important. It is not identical with any of the main families, the Alexandrian (the ' Neutral ' of Westcott and Hort) or the Western, into which the manuscript evidence has been classified by modern scholars. In Mark it clearly belongs rather to the family which Streeter identified as that used by Origen during his later years at Caesarea, and which is consequently named ' Caesarean ', though this manuscript strengthens the probability that the origin of this family was in Egypt, whence it may have been carried by Origen himself to Caesarea. In Luke and John the Caesarean text has not been identified, but the Chester Beatty manuscript corresponds to its general character, being intermediate between the Alexandrian and Western types of text, but slightly nearer to the former. In Acts it is distinctly of the Alexandrian type, having a few of the minor variants characteristic of the Western, but none of the major variants so noticeable in that book.

In the Pauline Epistles the differences between the two

families are less important, but the Chester Beatty MS. is again definitely, but not invariably, on the Alexandrian side. It is noteworthy that the Epistle to the Hebrews is plainly accepted as Pauline, being placed immediately after Romans. One notable variant is that the doxology to Romans (xvi. 25-27), which in the earlier manuscripts stands at the end of chapter xvi and in the great mass of later manuscripts at the end of chapter xiv, is here placed at the end of chapter xv. It is probable that the manuscript did not include the Pastoral Epistles, since the five leaves missing at the end would not have sufficed to hold them.

The Revelation papyrus agrees more with the four earliest of the vellum manuscripts than with the later ones, but is not closely attached to any of them.

The net result of this discovery—by far the most important since the discovery of the Sinaiticus—is, in fact, to reduce the gap between the earlier manuscripts and the traditional dates of the New Testament books so far that it becomes negligible in any discussion of their authenticity. No other ancient book has anything like such early and plentiful testimony to its text, and no unbiased scholar would deny that the text that has come down to us is substantially sound. On the other hand, it is evident that by the end of the second century variants in the minor details of the text were plentiful and widely diffused. It is clear that in the second century there was no general control of the text of the books which were gradually coming to be recognised as canonical. Manuscripts were copied in all parts of the world without comparison with one another, and often, no doubt, by untrained scribes. Hence mistakes and small variants easily arose and were repeated, and it was only gradually that they were submitted to control and revision. We must therefore accept minor uncertainties as to the details of the text, without pinning our faith wholly to any one of the recognised families ; but we have every right to be satisfied of its general integrity and its faithfulness as the record of the earliest Christian writings.

The Chester Beatty papyri have therefore strengthened very materially the basis—already very strong—of our confidence in the text of the New Testament as it has come down to us. For the dates and authenticity of the Gospels (a more important point for my present purpose) evidence of an even more striking character has been acquired within the last thirteen years. This is chiefly from a small scrap of papyrus received by the John Rylands Library from Professor Grenfell in 1920, but first identified and published by Mr. C. H. Roberts in 1935. It is a tiny fragment, measuring only about $3\frac{1}{2}$ by $2\frac{1}{4}$ inches, bearing on both sides of it portions of a few verses of the Fourth Gospel, ch. xviii. 31–33, 37, 38 ; but its importance lies in the fact that papyrological experts agree in assigning the date of its writing to the first half of the second century. Small therefore as it is, it suffices to prove that a manuscript of this Gospel was circulating, presumably in provincial Egypt where it was found, about the period A.D. 130–150. Allowing even a minimum time for the circulation of the work from its place of origin, this would throw back the date of composition so near to the traditional date in the last decade of the first century that there is no longer any reason to question the validity of the tradition.

And this evidence does not stand alone. In the same year, 1935, Dr. (now Sir) H. I. Bell and Mr. T. C. Skeat, of the British Museum, published some fragments, purchased the previous year for the Museum, of three leaves of a papyrus codex, the writing of which can also be ascribed to the first half of the second century. They contain records of incidents in our Lord's life, apparently forming portions of a Gospel differing from the four canonical books though with strong signs of relation to them. The style is simple and straightforward, without any of the exaggerations or tendentious doctrinal character of the later apocryphal gospels; and its date of origin must be assigned to the first century. The fragments include records of four incidents in our Lord's life. One of these is otherwise unknown: it is apparently a miracle wrought on the banks of the Jordan, but unfortunately the papyrus is so much mutilated that its exact character is uncertain. Two others report incidents also recorded in the Synoptic Gospels, one being the healing of the leper recorded in Mark i. 40–42, Matthew viii. 2–3, Luke v. 12–13; the other is the testing of our Lord with regard to the lawfulness of paying tribute to Caesar (Mark xii. 14–15, Matthew xxii. 17–18, Luke xxii. 21–25), but incorporating also Mark vii. 6–7, and Matthew xv. 7–9: "Why call ye me with your mouth Master, when ye hear not what I say? Well did Isaiah prophesy of you, saying, This people honoureth me with their lips, but their heart is far from me. In vain do they worship me, teaching as their doctrine the command-ments of men." The language of the Synoptic Gospels is evident here; but in the fourth incident the language of the Fourth Gospel is equally clear. It records a discussion with the rulers of the people, and runs as follows:

"Turning to the rulers of the people he spake this saying: Search (*or* ye search) the Scriptures, in which ye think that ye have life; these are they which bear witness of me. Think not that I came to accuse you to my Father; there is one that accuseth you, even Moses, on whom ye have set your hope. And when they said, we know well that God spake unto Moses, but as for thee we know not whence thou art, Jesus answered and said unto them, Now is your unbelief accused . . . And the

rulers laid their hands on him that they might take him
and hand him over to the multitude : and they could not
take him because the hour of his betrayal was not yet
come. But he himself, even the Lord, going forth out
of their hands, departed from them."

This is not a continuous excerpt from the Fourth Gospel,
but it contains phrases from John v. 39, 45, ix. 29, vii. 30,
x. 39, in the unmistakable style of that Gospel. It is evident
therefore that the writer of this " new Gospel " was
acquainted not only with the Synoptic Gospels but with
St. John : for the only alternative, that he was using
material which was afterwards incorporated in the Fourth
Gospel, is highly improbable in view of the very individual
style of that Gospel. There is no evidence or probability
of a school of " Johannine " writers earlier than the Gospel
itself.

Here, therefore, is confirmatory evidence of the existence
of the Fourth Gospel by about the end of the first century ;
and the implications of this evidence are of the first importance. If the Gospel was written before the end of the
first century, as seems now to be irrefragably proved, not
only are the contentions of Baur, van Manen, and all that
school shattered to pieces, but the probability of the authorship of the Apostle St. John seems to be enormously
strengthened. At the end of that Gospel is a certificate
(xxi. 24) written evidently by some persons who claimed to
speak with authority : " This is the disciple which testifieth
of these things, and wrote these things, and we know that
his testimony is true " ; and this disciple is identified above
(verse 20) as " the disciple whom Jesus loved, which also
leaned on his heart at supper, and said, Lord, which is he
that betrayeth thee ". The beloved disciple can only be St.
John ; for only the Twelve were present on that occasion

(Mark xiv. 17), and of the Twelve the three closest to our
Lord were Peter, James and John, and of these three Peter
was the interlocutor with the beloved disciple, and James
was dead long before the Gospel was written. Now if the
Gospel had been written after the middle of the second
century, such a certificate might perhaps be explained away
as a forger's attempt to authenticate his work, comparable
with the first-person expressions which appear to identify
the apocryphal Gospel of Peter as the work of that Apostle ;
but if it was written at the end of the first century, when
many persons were alive who could confirm or contradict it,
such an explanation is impossible. To say, as Bishop
Barnes does in a book which will be mentioned below, that
this chapter is a later addition, is wholly unjustifiable.
There is no scrap of evidence to support such an assertion,
which assumes that after the book had been circulating for
sixty or seventy years, far from the place of its origin, and
was already approaching or had already achieved (as we
know it had by the time of Irenaeus at latest) general
acceptance, some group of men thought it necessary to
append to it their certificate of authorship, and succeeded
in superseding and causing a complete obliteration of the
book as it had been current for two generations. Such a
claim, which invents evidence that does not exist and is
contrary to obvious probabilities, is surely negligible.

If, then, the Apostle St. John was indeed the author, how
much fruitless controversy is cut away ! Indeed, one
cannot see what interest the hostile critic has in denying
the authorship of St. John, when the only alternative is that
it is the work of some one else who lived at the same time
and was recognised by his contemporaries as having had
similar opportunities. Scholars must make their account
with the fact that we have in the Fourth Gospel the reminiscences by an eye-witness of facts and discourses, often

of a more intimate and private character than the public
utterances recorded by the Synoptics which formed the
staple material of Christian missionaries, expressed very
probably in a style acquired by the evangelist over his
length of years, but reflecting a direct knowledge which none
of the Synoptics could claim. On this view the numerous
phrases which imply the presence of an eye-witness fall into
place, such as the mentions of the names of the speakers in
conversation with our Lord. Thus in the narrative of the
feeding of the five thousand, where the Synoptics speak of
" They " or " The disciples ", the Fourth Gospel specifies
" Philip answered him ", and " Andrew, Simon Peter's
brother, saith unto him " (vi. 7, 8). Similarly Simon Peter
is named in vi. 68, Thomas in xi. 16, Philip and Andrew in
xii. 21, 22 ; in the long discourse in chapters xiii–xvi. Peter,
" the disciple whom Jesus loved " (if this were not the
writer, why is he not named ?), Peter again, Thomas, Philip
and Judas are mentioned by name ; and after the Resurrection Thomas, Peter, Nathaniel, the sons of Zebedee, the
beloved disciple, and again Peter. Are these to be regarded
as attempted dramatisation on the part of a writer in the
middle of the second century ? Is it not more reasonable
to take them at their face value as the recollections of an
eye-witness, who has probably often repeated these stories
to his hearers ? So also with the frequent topographical
details : " Bethany beyond Jordan " (i. 28), " Aenon near
to Salim " (iii. 23), Jacob's well at Sychar, near to the parcel
of ground that Jacob gave to his son Joseph (iv, 5), the
pool of Bethesda (v. 2), the boats from Tiberias (vi. 23),
Solomon's porch (x. 23), the place beyond Jordan where
John baptized (x. 40), Bethany about fifteen furlongs from
Jerusalem (xi. 18), the city called Ephraim in the country
near to the wilderness (xi. 54), the brook Cedron (xviii. 1),
the place called the Pavement (xix. 13). All this is surely

more natural as coming from the personal reminiscences of the writer than as an invention of over a century later and some eighty years after the destruction of Jerusalem and the practical evacuation of Palestine by the Jewish community.

Whatever may be thought of the argument in respect of the authorship, the combined evidence of the Rylands and New Gospel papyri seems to establish beyond reasonable doubt the first-century date of the Fourth Gospel, which carries with it dates farther back in that century for the Synoptic Gospels. This, if recognised, must become a cardinal point in the external history of the earliest Christian documents and the Apostolic Age, the importance of which will become still clearer in the following section.

3

DR. BARNES AND *THE RISE OF CHRISTIANITY*

IT would at any time have been of interest to draw the attention of students of the Bible to the new evidence which throws so much light upon it, and which so markedly tends to reassure them of the substantial integrity and trustworthiness of its record. That is indeed the main purpose of this book. But it seems all the more necessary to emphasise these results of recent research because of the appearance of the book by the Bishop of Birmingham, referred to above, entitled *The Rise of Christianity*. Issued under the name of a bishop, it may well have an influence much greater than I think it is entitled to on its own merits. I have no taste for controversy with one who holds so honourable a post in the Church of England ; but it would be cowardly for anyone writing or speaking on this subject to let the assertions of this book go unchallenged, or to allow it to be believed that they represent the results of up-to-date scholarship. They appear, on the contrary, to represent the frame of mind described above as dominant fifty or sixty years ago among scholars who regarded themselves as advanced. The book appears to me to show a very imperfect knowledge or appreciation of recent discoveries, and a thoroughly unscholarly attitude to evidence. So far from being the expression of unbiased examination, it is at least as one-sided and unscientific in its balance in one direction as the most hardened " fundamentalist " is in the other.

It seems therefore relevant to the purpose of this essay to devote some pages to a somewhat detailed examination of the statements and arguments in the Bishop's book. It

seems to me to be vitiated from beginning to end by an
unreasoning and unreasonable prejudice against the traditional view of the Bible, and a wholly unscholarly readiness
to accept the flimsiest argument against the traditional view,
and to ignore the weight of evidence on the other side.
The Bishop was, I believe, a distinguished mathematician,
but I can see no sign of the application of a rigorous mathe-
matical method in his treatment of evidence ; and the result
is that he asserts his belief in Christianity after discrediting
and cavilling at nearly all the evidence on which Christianity
is based.

It is essential to give some details which justify this
criticism.

The first sixty pages of the book are occupied by a sketchy
summary of the history of the ancient world, from palaeo-
lithic man to the Christian era.   It is largely irrelevent to
the main subject of the book, but it gives some foretaste
of what is to come by ignoring most of the evidence that
has come to light during the last two generations.   Thus no
mention is made of the discovery of the antiquity of writing,
so important as this is from its bearing on the authority
of the Pentateuch and of the narrative of the period of the
Judges.   No reference is made to the epoch-making discoveries of Ras Shamra, which disclose the literature of the
Canaanites at the time of the Hebrew invasion and provide
the background for the long struggle between the worships
of Jehovah and Baal which coloured the whole history of
the kingdoms of Israel and Judah.   Nothing is said of the
laws of the Hurri, and their parallelism with the laws of the
Pentateuch and consequent confirmation of the antiquity
of the latter.   It is the same with matters of smaller detail.
The date of Hammurabi is put at about 2100 B.C. (as in the
first edition of the Cambridge Ancient History, 1923), without indication that it has now been brought down to the

first half of the eighteenth century or (by some) even later ; and the date of the fall of Nineveh is given as 606 B.C., in ignorance of the Babylonian Chronicle published by Mr. C. J. Gadd in 1923, which definitely fixes it in a particular month of the year 612.

Coming to the New Testament, Dr. Barnes expresses surprise that " there is in classical literature written before A.D. 110 a practically complete silence as regards the new religion ". Of what authors is he thinking ? Which of the few who wrote within this period would have been likely to take much notice of one more of the Oriental cults which flowed into the city of Rome, and whose adherents, as Dr. Barnes admits, were mainly of an ill-educated lower middle class ? Tacitus (much of whose work is lost) mentions them as an " ingens multitudo " ; Suetonius refers to them ; and Pliny, writing only just outside the Bishop's period, deals with them at length. What more could reasonably be expected ?

Dr. Barnes begins his study of the Christian literature by roundly ruling out all miracles. He thus dismisses such cardinal beliefs of the Christian faith as the Virgin Birth, the Resurrection, and the Ascension, which must surely make very painful the recitation of the Apostles' and the Nicene Creeds. It also reduces much of the Gospel narrative to the level of legend. The birth stories " in the opinion of analytical scholars who accept modern scientific postulates, are not history, they are edifying legend ". The birth at Bethlehem " cannot be regarded as historical ". Nazareth is accepted as the place of birth, but hesitatingly, since some scholars think that the epithet " Nazarene " has nothing to do with the place Nazareth. Similarly the Crucifixion narratives are discredited. Some facts were no doubt easily remembered ; " but it is doubtful how far a number of other circumstances of his death can with confidence be accepted as historical ". They seem to have been written up from passages in the Psalms. This disposes of one utterance from the Cross, recorded by Matthew and Mark. Two of those recorded by Luke are questioned, since it is unlikely that " at the very end of such an exhausting death as crucifixion Jesus would have been able to cry loudly and articulately " ; while of the third it is sufficient to say that " analytical scholars conclude that the Lukan story of the two thieves is not to be regarded as historical ".

Distressing as it is to abandon belief in the Resurrection as a physical fact, " we cannot, out of deference to religious sentiment, reject the principle of the uniformity of nature which is fundamental in the outlook created by modern science ". Dr. Barnes is emphatic that " the resurrection is one of the great essential truths of Christianity " ; but he is equally emphatic that " this tenet of the Christian faith is quite independent of the question as to whether the body of Jesus was re-animated after his death. The disciples, it is admitted, were convinced that he was living and active among them ; but Dr. Barnes gives no explanation how they came to have this feeling so strongly, in so short a time after the tragedy of his death. Verbal differences in the narrative of the burial are treated as if they discredited the whole story ; but would not verbal identity have been far more suspicious ? As to the post-resurrection stories, they are " in the domain of religious romance not of religious history ". The moving story of the walk to Emmaus " is told with Luke's consummate skill, though we are left with the belief that it is not history, and that Luke himself did not give it as more than allegory ". How many unprejudiced readers of the narrative feel that ? Finally, the Ascension story is " naïvely pre-Copernican ". What else could it be ? The complete form of it is contained " in the editorial insertion in Acts (i. 3–11) ", apparently after A.D. 150; and no weight is to be attached to the traditional " forty days ", since forty was just a conventional number, meaning a considerable period, but with no precise significance.

A special word seems necessary with regard to the Last Supper. Dr. Barnes regards the narrative in Luke as embodying a different tradition from that followed by either Mark or Paul; and of the various forms of the Lukan text he prefers that of the ' Western ' authorities. I am inclined to believe that he is wrong in both respects. I think it can be shown that the only two primary authorities are Mark and Paul. Matthew follows Mark, and Luke is an amalgamation of Mark and Paul. And of the Lukan text, the normal criteria of textual criticism seem to show that the longer (Alexandrian) form is the original. Dr. Barnes does not say which form he prefers of the ' Western ' text. There are in fact five variations, two Latin and three Syriac; and it is this variety that tells against them. They seem to be different attempts to get rid of the difficulty caused by the mention, in the longer form, of two Cups.[1] If the ' Western ' text, in any of its forms, were the original, there is no reason why anyone should wish to alter it; but the difficulty of the Alexandrian form naturally invited alterations, which took different shapes in the Latin and Syrian churches.

This free handling of the Gospel narratives is necessarily dependent in part on the dates which Dr. Barnes assigns to the several books. His chronological scheme seems to depend largely on the date which he assigns to the Third Gospel. This, he argues, cannot have been written till after A.D. 94, because the writer names Lysanias as tetrarch of Abilene at the time when John the Baptist began his ministry

[1] See *The Ministry and the Sacraments* (Student Christian Union Press), 1937, pp. 272–86.

(Luke iii. 1).   Now Josephus mentions a Lysanias who was killed by Antony about 36 B.C., and later, when writing of events in the twelfth year of Claudius (A.D. 52), he refers to Abila as having been the tetrarchy of Lysanias (*Antiquities* xv. 4, 1, xx. 7, 1); hence Dr. Barnes argues that the author of the Third Gospel (not Luke, who must have died many years before), having read Josephus hastily, assumed that Lysanias was tetrarch in the fifteenth year of Tiberius (A.D. 28–29).   Consequently, since Josephus's *Antiquities* was published about A.D. 94, the Gospel must have been written after this date, about A.D. 100, " by a well-educated man, otherwise unknown ", using his material " with undue freedom . . . and occasionally careless in quoting from the information to which he had access ".   Matthew was produced about the same date, though with later editorial changes.   Mark was earlier, possibly about A.D. 75, but it might have been ten years later : it is not a historic biography, but a collection of anecdotes from many sources, re-edited more than once in the second century.   It is difficult to imagine an important conclusion being based on so slight a foundation.   It all rests on the assumption that Luke, in his exceptionally elaborate and detailed description of the date, was dependent on an inaccurate recollection of a " hastily read " (the adverb is several times repeated) passage of Josephus.   Because Josephus is the only source of our knowledge of the name Lysanias (except a mutilated inscription which shows that other persons of the name existed, but tells nothing about them), how is it justifiable to assume that no other source was open to Luke, and what weight ought this fantastic argument to carry against the natural interpretation of Luke's own preface, which implies that his narrative rests on a careful examination of the evidence of those who were eye-witnesses from the beginning ?

The weakness of Dr. Barnes's argument for the late dates

of the Synoptic Gospels is thus evident; and it breaks down altogether if the proof of the first-century date of the Fourth Gospel, set out in the previous section, is accepted; since it is universally agreed that the Synoptic Gospels must be earlier than the Fourth.

The whole of the Bishop's treatment of the Gospels is full of similarly weak arguments and dogmatic assertions for which the foundations are wholly inadequate. A few examples must be given to justify such a statement. It is admitted that the stories of the Nativity in Matthew and Luke differ so profoundly that they must have been written independently; yet it is immediately added that the contrasts between them would have been more glaring if " some process of harmonisation ", " some skilful removals of contradictions " had not taken place, probably during the second century, possibly between the years A.D. 140–175 —by which time Irenaeus, to whom the four canonical Gospels are the long-accepted foundation of the faith, was a grown man, perhaps fifty years old at the end of it. This assumption is quite gratuitous. Again, we are told that John apparently did not believe that Jesus was a descendant of David, because Jesus made no reply to the taunt " What, doth the Christ come out of Galilee ? " (John vii. 42); but how could he, since the words are not said to have been uttered in his presence ? Then a census of Palestine, in the time of Herod, as described by Luke, is said to be incredible; yet since 1893 there has been ample evidence of a system of fourteen-year censuses in the Roman Empire, and it is pure assumption that Judaea was excepted. There is also evidence (known since 1907) that persons were required to return to their original homes for the purpose of the census (how Dr. Barnes knows that Joseph's ancestors had left Bethlehem a thousand years before is not made clear). Since the Jews said to Jesus, ' Thou art not yet fifty

years old ', the probability is said to be ' fairly strong ' that
John thought of Jesus as nearly fifty years old ; and this is
said to be confirmed by the assertion of the Jews (not by
Jesus), ' Forty and six years was this temple in building.'
The express statement of Luke that he was thirty years old
is disallowed on the ground that the age of thirty had an
especial significance in Jewish history, since it was the age
of Joseph when he became prime minister and of David
when he became king !

Some of the Bishop's statements are almost incredibly
erratic. Thus with regard to the Virgin Birth he says that
the author of the Fourth Gospel " pointedly ignores it,
and twice over refers to Jesus as the son of Joseph " ; but
as he does not refer to the birth at all, the ignoring is not
very pointed, and the references to Jesus as the son of
Joseph are not by John at all, but in one case by Philip
and in the other by the Jews (John i. 45, vii. 42), none of
whom could have spoken of him otherwise. Still more
surprising is the assertion that " in the earliest tradition
preserved by Mark, Mary seems throughout unconscious
of her son's divine origin and destiny " : the fact being
that Mary is not mentioned in that Gospel at all, except in
the statement that " his brethren and his mother, standing
without, sent unto him ".

It is suggested that " it would not have been deemed
beyond reason to say that a man was son of God " ; but is
there any evidence that this was done, except in the case
of the imperial family ? Dr. Barnes quotes no other instances ; and it was certainly not thought admissible to
attribute divinity to Herod (Acts xii. 23). It is flatly laid
down that the phrase in the introduction to the Fourth
Gospel, " The Word was God " (Θεός ἦν ὁ Λόγος) does not
mean that the Word was God, but that he was with God
and partook of His nature without being identical with

Him ; but θεὸς is not the same as θεῖος. The Logos-doctrine and the Virgin Birth are said to be incompatible ; " the virgin birth of traditional dogma ought to have pro-duced [*sic*] a semi-divine being, half God and half man ".

The Bishop is naturally attracted (as some other scholars have been) by the statement (in a late epitome of Church history, apparently based upon Philip of Side, a writer of the fifth century) that Papias affirmed that " John ὁ θεολόγος and James his brother were slain by the Jews ". He admits that one would have expected James to be described as ' son of Zebedee ' (and surely still more one would have expected the pair to be described as ' sons of Zebedee '), and is inclined to accept the (entirely unsupported) con-jecture of " some scholars " that the passage originally ran " killed James and John with the sword ". This suffices him to " conclude that in all probability John the apostle, the son of Zebedee, was martyred with his brother James in A.D. 44 ". But to arrive at this " probability " he has to ignore the general tradition, going back to Irenaeus, who had it from Polycarp, St. John's disciple, and to Polycrates, bishop in the latter part of the second century, that John lived and died in Ephesus, and the fact of Polycarp's discipleship, which would have been impossible if John had died twenty-five years before Polycarp was born. It is also observable that Papias did not say that John and James were slain by the Jews *at the same time* ; and even if the repeated description of Papias himself as a disciple of John is to be questioned (as it is by Eusebius), he would hardly have included John among the disciples of our Lord whose sayings he diligently collected at second hand if he had believed that he had died a century or more before. It is only by the quite illegitimate falsification of the text, men-tioned above, that Dr. Barnes evades the obvious argument that if the two brothers had been martyred at the same time, it is incredible that the author of Acts would have recorded the death of James and not that of John. In any other connection the Bishop would surely not have so misjudged on which side the weight of evidence lies.

With all this destructive criticism, it must be freely recognised that Dr. Barnes throughout expresses the highest appreciation of the character and teaching of Jesus. " The central fact of Christianity is, and always has been, Jesus. Upon him, upon men's belief in the truth of his teaching and the divine beauty of his character, the Christian movement was, and continues to be, based. . . . The teaching of Jesus as to God's nature and as to man's duty and destiny, the loyalty of Jesus to his teaching, the example of Jesus as he went to the cross, and, above all, the certainty of his knowledge of God,—these facts are fundamental to Christianity. . . . The Christian faith continues to exist because men still feel that of Jesus it was truly said that ' never man spake like this man '. To him they continue to come, saying ' Thou hast the words of eternal life ' ; and, coming, they worship him with the old words, ' Thou art the Christ, the Son of God '." With the old *words*, but, so far as the Bishop is concerned, apparently not with the old meaning. There is no reason to question Dr. Barnes's sincerity in his devotion to Christianity as he sees it ; and with the theological implications of his disbelief in the Divine birth and Resurrection this inquiry is not concerned. The gravamen of the charge against him is that he has cut away all the grounds on which the traditional faith of Christians is based, and that his arguments for doing so are thoroughly unsound in respect of scholarship. He relegates nearly the whole of the Christian literature to the second century ; he rejects much of its record as legend and untrustworthy ; he leaves an unfilled gap of two generations between our Lord's life and the records of it. Beyond his picture of the " peasant artisan " of Galilee, with a love of nature and of children, he gives little indication of the positive teaching which he accepts or the means by which he distinguishes it from that which he regards as unauthentic. Apparently every reader is free to pick and choose from the record such teaching and such sayings as he finds acceptable, and to reject the rest as the additions of later generations. It is an eclectic creed, based on shifting and unsound foundations.

For the Gospel records he has very little respect, and the criteria are equally subjective. He would even suggest uncertainty as to the trustworthiness of the text as it has been handed down. " It must never be forgotten that . . . none of our existing manuscripts of the New Testament goes back beyond the fourth century of our era." In view of the discovery of the Chester Beatty papyri, this is simply untrue. There is a grudging admission that earlier fragments have been found, but no recognition of the scale or importance of these fragments. It would have been more true to say that it must never be forgotten that we now have substantial portions of the Gospels, Acts and Revelation, and an almost complete manuscript of the Pauline Epistles, going back to the beginning of the third century, which in spite of verbal variations not affecting doctrine guarantee the integrity of the tradition and the substantial trustworthiness of the record of the texts of the books as they originally took shape. As to the dates at which they took their final shape, Dr. Barnes holds views which modern discoveries show to be unsound. His relegation of all to the second century is refuted by the evidence of the Rylands fragment of St. John ; and his repeated suggestions of alterations, insertions and re-editings up to the middle of the second century have no justification on grounds of reasonable scholarship or bibliographical probability. " We cannot too often remind ourselves " that the textual foundations of the New Testament record are quite exceptionally sound.

Dr. Barnes still further undermines the foundations of Christianity by minimising the duration of our Lord's ministry. He claims that it did not begin until our Lord was nearly fifty years of age, and it lasted for about a year (perhaps no more than a few months) in Galilee and the passover week in Jerusalem. How the dates of birth and death are to be adjusted does not appear. Dr. Barnes allows that the Fourth Gospel records three passovers : but this Gospel " gives us religious symbolism rather than history. It is a sustained allegory rather than a record of fact. Thus, though it mentions three passovers . . . there is always the possibility that the writer has created the longer period for some symbolic reason which we do not now perceive ", —and which through all these nineteen centuries no one has perceived. Surely this is, in the strict sense of the term, imbecility of scholarship !

So much, for the present, of Dr. Barnes's treatment of the Gospels. The other books are treated in the same cavalier fashion, with assertions of late dates, re-editings, insertions and general corruption to suit his subjective views. He says that the first dozen chapters of Acts consist of history mixed with improbable legends. The resurrection story in the first chapter is an editorial insertion probably made towards the middle of the second century. The early speeches, though probably embodying early traditions, are doubtless free compositions of the author. One would be glad to know what are the early traditions thus embodied if they are not the repeated affirmations of the Resurrection, the Divine Sonship, and " the miracles, wonders and signs " wrought by him. The common authorship of Acts and the third Gospel is recognised, but the author was not Luke : he used the travel-diary of Paul's physician but he was almost certainly not that physician, and in fact had probably not known Paul personally. The narrative of Paul's early life is unreliable. He was " emphatically not a manual-worker, but like a well-to-do clergyman or professor who might speak of working in his vegetable garden "; though he repeatedly refers to maintaining himself by the work of his own hands (Acts xx. 34 ; 1 Cor. iv. 12 ; 2 Cor. xi. 9 ; 1 Thess. ii. 9 ; 2 Thess. iii. 8). The narrative of his speech in Jerusalem is almost certainly fictitious. Between Paul and Peter, it is roundly affirmed there was no reconciliation ; and there was obviously fierce rivalry between Paul and Apollos, though the narrative in Acts says nothing of the sort. Of the Epistles, parts (but only parts) of Romans are genuine ; 1 Corinthians is an amalgam of leaflets and portions of letters ; in particular the narrative of the Last Supper is a tract written late in the first century, and attached with alterations to the Corinthian letter ; the passage on the Resurrection is one of the many tracts or fly-sheets written one or two generations after him ; the prose-poem on Love is totally unlike his style, and shows a literary excellence not found in any other passage attributed to him. In 2 Corinthians two letters have been joined together in the wrong order (this view, of course, is not peculiar to Dr. Barnes), but much is genuine ; Galatians is apparently accepted ; Ephesians is a mosaic of fragments of Paul, but not Pauline in style (then why are the fragments said to be his, and why is the suggestion, ascribed to " many scholars ", that it belongs to a later generation, apparently welcomed ?) ; Colossians, Philippians and Philemon are " genuine or partially genuine " ; Philippians seems to be a composition of fragments of two letters, joined together (with that perversity which seems to beset editors) in reverse order. 1 Thessalonians is said to bear every mark of genuineness, except that the passage on the Second Coming

D

may be a later insertion; 2 Thessalonians may well be the
work of an imitator.   The Pastoral Epistles are placed after
A.D. 144, on the ground that the words in 1 Timothy vi. 20
translated in the Authorised Version "oppositions of
science" should be rendered "antitheses of gnosis", and
are a warning against the work of Marcion (who was
expelled from the Church about that date), entitled *Antitheses*.   Marcion is known to have made a collection of ten
epistles of Paul, and this was probably the first collection
cf them, made about A.D. 140.

Of the other Epistles, Hebrew is certainly non-Pauline,
but its date and author are unknown.   The epistles ascribed
to Peter are not genuine; the first was written about A.D. 80
by an unknown Jewish Christian, the second about A.D. 150.
Jude is dated about A.D. 130.   The Epistles of John are
probably by the same writer as the Gospel.   Lastly, Revelation, in its final form, was probably written at the end of
the first century, by a John who was not the apostle, and
not the author of the Fourth Gospel.

It will have been noticed that in his analysis of the New
Testament books, Dr. Barnes is very free with his suggestions of editorial revisions, of insertions, and of the
composition of scattered fragments into the books as they
have descended since the middle of the second century.
He is by no means alone in this habit, which is only too
common among critics of the Bible; but it shows a lack
of realisation of bibliographical probabilities.   There is no
doubt that there were, about the middle of the first century,
a number of documents relating to the life of Jesus, either
narratives of incidents, such as we find in the Gospel of
Mark, or collections of discourses, such as that known as
Q, the existence of which is generally assumed as the source
of passages common to Matthew and Luke, but not found
in Mark.   Luke expressly testifies to the existence of such

writings, and they formed the materials out of which the synoptists compiled their Gospels. But this is very different from the picture of a welter of fragments, tracts, leaflets, letters, which during the first half of the second century coagulated somehow into the books as we now know them. The question must be faced. How did these *disjecta membra* exist? How were they preserved, and how were they brought together? Dr. Barnes himself asks these questions with regard to the Pauline epistles: "Who gathered together these letters of Paul? Where had they been in the meantime? . . . Were they in rolls, or, as is more probable, in book form [1]? Had scattered pages been tied up with other early Christian tracts, sermon-notes, or fly-sheets? How did the man, or men, who published the material determine what in it was actually from Paul?" These are very pertinent questions, but the Bishop provides no answer. Why should none of the original documents be preserved intact, especially the letters addressed to particular churches? Who would have ventured to mutilate them, and who had authority to put the fragments together and edit them and attach to them the name of Paul? What central authority issued them, and imposed them on the whole Christian world, in Europe, Asia and Africa? And when a book (*e.g.* Acts) was once formed, how were insertions made in it, or new editions substituted for the original? In the case of Acts there is indeed evidence of somewhat free rehandling by someone who thought himself entitled to give variant versions of certain details, and these have survived in certain Western manuscripts: but this

---

[1] It is not clear why he thinks this more probable. It is, in fact contrary to all bibliographical knowledge or probability. So far no manuscript in codex form has come to light as early as the first century, and even the larger epistles come well within the established limits of a papyrus roll, and would be impossibly short for a codex.

is a very small matter compared with the rehandling and re-editing envisaged by the Bishop, the external evidence of which has completely disappeared. This light-hearted ignoring of bibliographical possibilities and probabilities, whether by Dr. Barnes or others, is a sign of a lack either of knowledge or of thoroughness of thought. Dr. Barnes is fond of referring to " modern scholars " or " analytic scholars " as supporting the views which he holds ; but the support is purely illusive, since he never quotes their names. There are no means, therefore, of checking their quality or their quantity or their date ; and the reader is never told how many other " modern " or " analytic " scholars hold different views. It is another example of the fatal error of taking into account only the evidence which is in favour of one's own views, and ignoring that which tells against them. The bibliography of " books which may be consulted " gives no help in this respect. Of the 67 works mentioned ten are earlier in date than 1900 ; 42 lie between 1900 and 1930 ; and only 14 and part of another are later than 1930, ten of which have very little to do with the main subject of the book. Several of them are by authors such as Lightfoot, Hort, Headlam, Gore, Sanday, Gwatkin, Ramsay, who certainly did not share Dr. Barnes's views, and many others, such as the works of Eddington, Jeans, Planek, Fisher, Dill, Myres, Childe, Hall, Bury, Murray, Bevan, Heitland, Stuart Jones, have little or no bearing on his main critical contentions. For them his bibliography provides little support indeed   Lightfoot's *Essays on Supernatural Religion*, which would have been particularly relevant, is not mentioned at all.

The last-named work would have been particularly relevant to the next section of Dr. Barnes's book, which deals with the writers of the second century, though it would not give much support to his conclusions. He is favourably inclined to the Didache, apparently because of its differences from the canonical record and the tradition, particularly with regard to the Eucharist. It is affirmed that it probably passed through several editions, but no indication is given of what the proof is. Ultimately it was discarded because its account of the Last Supper was incompatible with that in 1 Corinthians and the Gospels. But why should its version be preferred to theirs ? Justin, who gives substantially the New Testament account, says that the Last Supper was imitated in the mysteries of Mithra ; and Dr. Barnes twists this into an affirmation of " the close affinity between the Mithraic communion and the form of Christian eucharist which ousted the primitive communion of the Didache". But if the Mithraic ritual was imitated from the Christian (and Dr. Barnes gives no reason for reversing Justin's evidence), it would indicate that the New Testament version, and not that of the Didache, was the prevalent practice, and would give no support to the view, to which Dr. Barnes evidently inclines, that Mithraism and the mystery religions in general had much influence on the development of Christianity. He argues rather oddly that there was acute rivalry between Mithraism and Christianity in the second and third centuries, and *therefore* if the one had a particular rite the other would be sure to copy it ; and he assumes, without evidence, that Christianity was the copyist.

The Ignatian letters lend themselves to criticism, because of the different forms in which they have come down to us, —the three in the Syriac version published by Cureton, the seven in the Greek version published by Voss and generally accepted since Lightfoot's exhaustive examination of them, and the fifteen in the Long Recension which is universally discarded as a late falsification. Dr. Barnes prefers the shorter Greek version, but considers that even

this must be referred to a date thirty or forty years later
than Ignatius, apparently *because* these letters imply that the
Gospels and several of the Epistles were already accepted
as authoritative, and because of the emphasis laid in them
on the importance of the episcopate. This is another
example of the acceptance or rejection of evidence according
as it does or does not support conclusions already arrived
at. The former argument breaks down with the now
established first-century date of the Gospels ; the latter
must remain as a debatable point in the history of ecclesi-
astical organisation, but cannot be disallowed by assuming
the contrary in advance. Especially is it inadmissible
simply to ignore the exhaustive treatment of the subject
by Lightfoot.

The Epistle of Polycarp is accepted as genuine, and it is
admitted to show a knowledge of most of the writings of
the New Testament ; but it is assigned to a date shortly
after the middle of the second century. In support of this
it is stated that " many scholars " (unspecified, as always)
think that there has been in its chapter xiii an interpolation
to recommend the letters of Ignatius ; that is, the evidence
is disallowed because its effect is unwelcome. Why should
anyone have been wishing to buttress up the letters of
Ignatius, which were not then questioned ? Ignatius is,
moreover, also mentioned in chapters ix and xiv ; and it is
incredible that Polycarp should, after A.D. 150, have been
asking for news of Ignatius and his companions, who had
been martyred some forty years before. Harnack, after
a long discussion, decides in favour of a date between
A.D. 110 and 117, or at any rate before 125. Polycarp's
letter, as it stands, testifies both to the general knowledge and acceptance of the New Testament books
round about A.D. 110, and to the genuineness of the
Ignatian letters ; and his testimony cannot be invalidated

merely because its trend is not that which Dr. Barnes wishes.

It is not necessary, however, to labour the point any further. Dr. Barnes's conclusion is that " we have no certain witness to the epistles of Paul earlier than Marcion, say in A.D. 140. About the same time the gospels became authoritative. The New Testament, as we have it, indicates the limits to speculative Christian theology which were maintained by the church's leaders towards the middle of the second century." Dr. Barnes does not say who these leaders were : and he appears to envisage a unified organisation of the Church which did not then exist. If the leadership were in Ephesus, how did Ephesus impose its conclusions on Alexandria and Antioch and Rome ? Did it then produce for the first time Gospels and Epistles previously unknown ? Or, if they previously existed in shorter forms, how were the enlarged and sophisticated forms imposed and given universal currency ? The whole process of the production of these books is compressed into an impossibly narrow space, between about A.D. 110 and 150. It does not make sense.

It does not seem necessary to follow the Bishop further, as he strains out meticulously every traditional gnat, while swallowing without a qualm any number of anti-traditional camels. It is sufficient to warn the reader that he has in the Bishop's book, not the results of the latest scholarship, but only a belated revival of a long-discredited school of criticism, which in no way invalidates the conclusions of more recent scholarship, as I have tried to set them out in the preceding section of this book. Dr. Barnes himself ends almost on a note of despair. The story of Christianity is " a most strange tale, which would be incredible if it were not true. . . . There emerged in Galilee a peasant artisan, . . . who felt that he knew God and was called

to serve Him.   This man for a brief year or so taught in
a remote district. . . .   Finally, because of teaching which
expressed his loyalty to God, he was executed as a common
criminal.   All memory of him ought rapidly to have
vanished."   But it did not.   "A new religion grew up,
ethical monotheism centred on Jesus the Christ."   After
being persecuted for wellnigh three centuries, it triumphed,
and immediately the salt went out of it.   An opportunist
monotheism, at its best Stoic rather than Christian, re-
mained.   Yet Christianity continues !   One may well ask
why and how ?   Dr. Barnes has in fact cut away nearly all
the foundations of the Christian faith, and then affirms his
belief in it.   He has reduced it to a year, or less, of the life
of a peasant artisan in Galilee and its neighbourhood, with
a week in Jerusalem ending in his death.   Of this life we
have no record for some two generations, and that record,
when produced, has been falsified by the most far-reaching
inventions and corruptions.   Within the next generation
that falsified record has established itself throughout the
Roman world.   It maintains itself as a persecuted faith for
less than two centuries ;   then it triumphs,—and is instantly
corrupted.   Yet it survives, and sixteen centuries later has
power to command the adherence of Dr. Barnes.   "Credit
quia incredibile."   Dr. Barnes should surely be glad to feel
that the grounds for his scepticism have been cut away by
recent discoveries, and that the interval between the life of
Jesus on earth and the records of it which have reached us
is much smaller than he has supposed.   This can be claimed
to be established now by objective evidence.   It is time to
brush away finally the cobwebs spun so thickly by Baur and
his followers ;   to profit from the exhaustive testing of the
foundations of the Christian tradition which the challenge
of that school brought forth, and from the new discoveries
of the present century ;   and to consider how the Bible

stands now, in the light of the latest additions to our knowledge and the interpretation of them in accordance with such critical examination as would be applied to other records of the past.

4

CRITICISM AND THE BIBLE

THE present generation is, to a greater extent than is often realised, better placed than its predecessors for applying a sane criticism to the study of the Bible. It is free alike from the conventional assumptions of the pre-critical age and from the anti-traditional assumptions of the ultra-sceptical school which exhausted itself in the latter part of the nineteenth century. It can strike a balance between these extremes. It is in no way bound to assume that the tradition which satisfied uncritical generations is exempt from criticism, nor, on the other hand, that the anti-traditional is always to be preferred, even though the bulk of the evidence is on the other side. Such a view is not merely a reaction against a period of excessive scepticism. It is ballasted by a considerable mass of ascertained fact, the result of archaeological and literary research during the past fifty years. It can therefore approach the evidence from a new and firmer standpoint. It can give tradition its due weight. It is less free than it was to spin cobwebs out of its own inner consciousness ; it has more facts to check them by, and has to form its theories under the salutary consciousness that more facts may at any time come to light to test them.

The attitude of the scholar to tradition has to be rectified. It is not only in the field of Biblical study that the value of tradition has been vindicated in recent years. Classical studies, especially in the field of Homeric criticism, have gone through a phase of exaggerated scepticism, which infected even the naturally more conservative British scholars, and have gradually come back to a healthier estimate of the value of tradition and a saner weighing of probabilities. Tradition is a bad master, but is a useful guide, and the scholar must teach himself not to be afraid of it. It is by no means always to be accepted, but it should always be scrutinised with respect ; and it should be realised that the early Christian centuries were not wholly credulous, nor deficient in critical ability.

A few instances may serve to illustrate this point. The Gospel of Peter circulated in the diocese of Antioch at the end of the second century. It claims the authorship of the Apostle Peter, and shows connection with the canonical Gospels. Prima facie appearances may therefore be said to be in its favour, and it was uncritically accepted as authentic narrative. But on being scrutinised it appears (1) that it is strongly tinged with hostility to the Jews, and has marks of the heresy of Docetism, which taught that our Lord's sufferings were only apparent and not real, (2) that it was condemned and suppressed as heretical by the bishop who found it in use in his diocese, (3) that there is no evidence of its existence before the middle of the second century, (4) that Eusebius unhesitatingly condemns it as spurious. Here, therefore, the adverse evidence is sufficient to outweigh the tradition which gave it temporary vogue in a part of the Christian world, and secured its continued existence at any rate to about the sixth century.

Coming to the Canon itself, there is the Second Epistle of Peter. This also claims the authorship of the Apostle, and secured a somewhat hesitating acceptance in the early Church. The tradition in its favour is therefore stronger. But it was not universally accepted by the early Fathers. Eusebius rejected it as unauthentic, though he says that it was regarded as useful by many and was studied with the other Scriptures. It was not included in the canon of the

Syrian Church. It contains a passage nearly identical with a passage in the Epistle of Jude, and, though opinion is not unanimous, most scholars hold Jude to be the original. There is therefore weighty evidence in this case against the tradition, and most scholars decide against the authenticity. Harnack makes it the one exception to his general acceptance of the traditional dates and authorships of the New Testament books, based upon an exceptionally full and exhaustive study of the early literature of Christianity.

Making a step further inside the Canon, we come to the Fourth Gospel. Here the tradition is unanimous in favour of its authenticity, and of the authorship of the Apostle John. Yet not a few modern scholars, including some who fully recognise and value the authority of the Gospel, doubt this ascription. Among English scholars, Streeter, Stanton, Turner, Burney and others decide against it, though by no means questioning its spiritual value. Here it must be said that modern discoveries, which have proved the existence of the Gospel in the first years of the second century, have powerfully reinforced the tradition, by showing that the express attribution of its authorship, in the final chapter, to the Beloved Disciple, must have been made at a time when there were many persons living who could confirm or deny its accuracy. Scholars remain free to form their own judgment ; but they are bound now to attach serious weight to the tradition, and to realise that thought may have moved more rapidly than they have been inclined to admit. Two-thirds of a century, uncontrolled by any accepted Canon of authoritative documents, left ample room for the initiation of trains of thought which took more pronounced forms in the second century ; and symptoms of such tendencies in some writings in the New Testament must be taken as proofs, not of the lateness of these writings, but of the earliness of these trains of thought.

Finally we may take the case of the Apocalypse. Here there was much hesitation in early times in admitting its canonicity. It did not appear in the original Canons of the Syrian and Egyptian churches, but in the West and by the Asiatic Fathers it was generally accepted unhesitatingly as the work of the Apostle John. Dionysius of Alexandria, in the third century, was the first to declare on grounds of style that it could not be the work of the author of the Fourth Gospel. On this ground most modern scholars agree with him; but the strength of the tradition on the other side must be recognised. In any case the date and authenticity of it are not affected by these doubts. The author gives his name as John, but he nowhere claims apostolicity or any particular authority. He is the transmitter of visions and messages that have been vouchsafed to him. Eusebius rather tentatively identifies him with the presbyter John mentioned by Papias, but there is no proof of this.

The point which it is desired to make here is that early Church tradition, though it must be weighed, must be recognised as weighty, and that its weight has been increased by the proof which archaeology has brought of the early date of the New Testament books. Scholars must free themselves from the obsession that the presumption is against the traditional. They must recognise that the presumption, though not immune from question, is the other way; and in this light they can go forward to apply to the New Testament books the critical principles which have been found valid in other fields of scholarship.

If fair play is thus given to them, it must be recognised that the New Testament books stand in a very strong position, the strength of which has been increased by recent discoveries and investigations. Short of the discovery of first-century manuscripts, their traditional first-century dates are confirmed by as strong evidence as it is reasonable to expect ; and with the shortening of the period the probabilities, and even the possibilities, of extensive corruption or rehandling are greatly reduced. And the links which connect our present New Testament with the first century are very strong. By the time of Irenaeus (c. A.D. 125–200) the canon of the New Testament, apart from doubts affecting a few books, is practically assured ; and one strong link, that of Polycarp (c. A.D. 70–155), connects Irenaeus with the age, and, in all probability, the person of St. John. There are many points affecting the exact dates and methods of composition of the several books, with which scholars rightly concern themselves ; but their function now is to elucidate, not to discredit or destroy.

It must be recognised also that, if the Fourth Gospel has to be placed not later than A.D. 95, and the Gospels of Matthew and Luke come before that, and Mark, which they utilise, before that again, the time for elaborate development is very much limited. The interval between the Crucifixion and St. Mark's gospel may be about the space of one generation, from about A.D. 30 to about A.D. 65. From that period a good many years must be cut off at the beginning, before the need for written records was felt. There is simply not time for the elaborate processes required for Dibelius' *Formgeschichte*, which has won rather surprising popularity, but which presupposes, first the dissemination of stories of the life and teaching of Jesus, then their collection and classification into groups according to their character, and then the formation of continuous narratives in which they were utilised. And all this in a world where communications were slow and Christian communities were scattered groups. There is simply not time for elaborate processes of literary workmanship and development. We have to be content with an altogether simpler procedure, suitable to a world where Christians were grouped in scattered communities, linked rather precariously in a world which was indifferent if it was not hostile. The details of the development of Christian literature we cannot know, and must not invent too much. What we are entitled to claim is that the books which we know as canonical were produced within some fifty years of the first century, and that the evidence for their text is in all essentials early and good. There is much room for diversities of interpretation, but the foundations stand sure, and we can without misgiving believe that we have in them the words of eternal life, to be interpreted and applied as best we can.